MAKING TOOLS
IN THE WILD

DEVI PURI

PowerKiDS
press.

New York

Published in 2016 by The Rosen Publishing Group, Inc.
29 East 21st Street, New York, NY 10010

First Edition

Editor: Sarah Machajewski
Book Design: Michael J. Flynn

Photo Credits: Cover (man) Alexander Walter/The Image Bank/Getty Images; cover, pp. 1, 3–4, 6, 8, 10, 12, 14, 16–18, 20, 22–24 (map background) Sergei Drozd/Shutterstock.com; p. 4 eduard ionescu/Shutterstock.com; p. 5 Andersen Ross/Blend Images/Getty Images; p. 7 gpointstudio/Shutterstock.com; p. 8 gorillaimages/Shutterstock.com; p. 9 kanin.studio/Shutterstock.com; p. 10 Pavel L Photo and Video/Shutterstock.com; p. 11 Andersen Ross/Iconica/Getty Images; p. 13 John Burke/Photodisc/Getty Images; p. 15 courtesy of U.S. Forest Service Northern Region Flickr; p. 16 Poonkasem Wiankaonoi/Shutterstock.com; p. 17 Portland Press Herald/Getty Images; p. 19 courtesy of cabs_1 Flickr; p. 21 Chayut Thanapochoochoung/Shutterstock.com; p. 22 James Ross/Taxi/Getty Images.

Library of Congress Cataloging-in-Publication Data

Names: Puri, Devi.
Title: Making tools in the wild / Devi Puri.
Description: New York : PowerKids Press, 2016. | Series: Wilderness survival skills | Includes index.
Identifiers: ISBN 9781508143277 (pbk.) | ISBN 9781508143284 (6 pack) | ISBN 9781508143291 (library bound)
Subjects: LCSH: Wilderness survival–Juvenile literature. | Survival–Juvenile literature.
Classification: LCC GV200.5 P87 2016 | DDC 613.6'9–dc23

Manufactured in the United States of America

CPSIA Compliance Information: Batch #BW16PK: For Further Information contact Rosen Publishing, New York, New York at 1-800-237-9932

CONTENTS

A NOTE TO READERS

Always talk with a parent or teacher before proceeding with any of the activities found in this book.
Some activities require adult supervision.

A NOTE TO PARENTS AND TEACHERS

This book was written to be informative and entertaining. Some of the activities in this book require adult supervision. Please talk with your child or student before allowing them to proceed with any wilderness activities. The authors and publisher specifically disclaim any liability for injury or damages that may result from use of information in this book.

FACING WILDERNESS CHALLENGES

From the time the first humans lived on Earth, people have dealt with nature's **challenges**—and there are many of them. Bad weather, deadly plants and animals, and tough **terrain** are just a few examples of challenges people have had to survive.

Over time, people started making tools that made it easier to survive in the **wilderness**. If you're a young wilderness adventurer, it's important to know how to make and use many kinds of tools.

This book will cover tools that are easy to bring with you into the wilderness, as well as how to make tools from **materials** found in your **environment**.

WHAT'S A SURVIVAL SKILL?

Anyone who enters the wilderness must be prepared to face whatever comes their way. It's important to build up survival skills before spending time in the wilderness. A survival skill is anything that helps you stay alive in a dangerous, or unsafe, **situation**.

Survival skills include building **shelter**, making fire, reading maps, and giving first aid. Knowing how to make tools is an important survival skill, too. You can build and make tools to help you survive a few hours or even a few days in the wilderness.

SURVIVAL TIP

Books and the Internet are great places to learn about survival skills. Spend some time researching at your library or online.

Always practice your survival skills before heading into the wilderness—it could be the difference between life and death.

WHAT TO BRING

Here's one important rule: always bring tools when you go into the wilderness. This will make your life much easier in a survival situation, because you won't have to spend time or **energy** making tools.

Many people agree that a knife is the most important tool you can have. You can use it to cut, chop, and **spear** pretty much anything. You should also bring tools to make water clean for drinking, tools for making fire, and a compass, which is a tool that shows directions.

HELPFUL WILDERNESS TOOLS

- KNIFE
- COMPASS
- MAP
- TOOLS TO MAKE WATER CLEAN
- FIRE-STARTING TOOLS, SUCH AS MATCHES AND PIECES OF PAPER
- FIRST-AID KIT
- FLASHLIGHT
- SMALL MIRROR
- ROPE

Here's a list of tools that can be very helpful in the wilderness. Be careful when handling unsafe objects, such as knives or fire-starting tools.

TIME TO IMPROVISE

Even if you've prepared and brought your own tools, something may happen that makes you unable to use them. Being without tools can feel scary, but this is when your survival skills will come in handy. You can **improvise** all kinds of tools using materials found in your environment.

Look around for things that can help you. Vines and plant matter can be used to make rope. Sharp objects can be used to make cutting tools. Sticks can help you create fire.

A walking stick is one of the easiest tools to find in the wilderness— just find a stick that's about your height. It can be used for support while you're walking, to create a path through overgrown plants, or to keep animals away.

KNIFE 101

The first tool you should make is a knife. A knife has two parts—a blade and a handle. Make the knife blade using stone or even bone. If you can find glass, plastic, or metal, these can be used, too.

Next, use a chipping tool to break off small pieces of your blade. You want to make it thin enough to act as a knife. Then, use a flaking tool to break off tiny pieces until you create a sharp edge. However, keep in mind that this would not work with plastic, glass, or metal.

SURVIVAL TIP

Use your knife or flaking tool for whittling, or carving wood. Whittling turns branches into sharp wooden tools, such as a spear or a **skewer**.

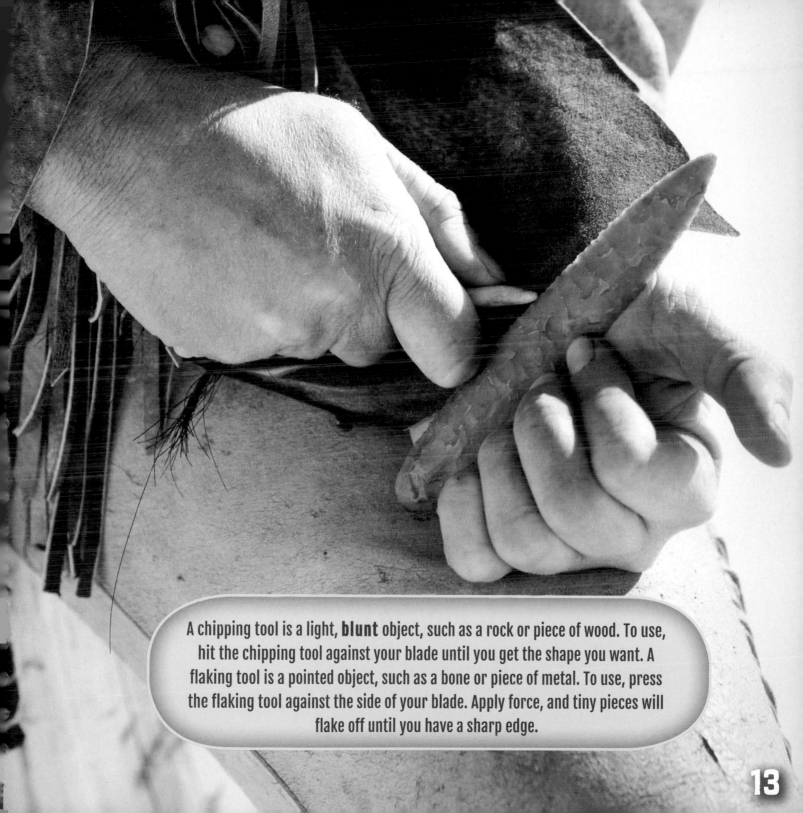

A chipping tool is a light, **blunt** object, such as a rock or piece of wood. To use, hit the chipping tool against your blade until you get the shape you want. A flaking tool is a pointed object, such as a bone or piece of metal. To use, press the flaking tool against the side of your blade. Apply force, and tiny pieces will flake off until you have a sharp edge.

THE IMPORTANCE OF CORDAGE

Once you have a blade, you need to find a handle. Use any object that can fit in your hand, such as a light piece of wood. But without tape or glue, what can you use to hold the blade and handle together? Cordage, or rope, is a good option.

Cordage can be made from the roots, stems, and leaves of many plants. To make cordage, simply braid long, flat **fibers** together. You can also twist the fibers between your hands in a method called twining.

SURVIVAL TIP

Cordage can be made from grass, straw, dogsbane, cattail leaves, nettle, willow bark, tree vines, and more.

Cordage is one of the most important survival tools. It can be used to build shelter and animal traps. It can be used to make other tools, such as a bow drill, which is used to make fire.

15

MAKING FIRE

Fire is important in survival situations, but you need tools to make it. If you don't have matches or a lighter, you can use materials found in your environment.

Make a hand drill from a stick, tree bark, and a wooden board. Make a V-shaped cut on the side of the board, and place the bark under it. Make a hole next to the V, and place the stick, or spindle, in the hole. A bow drill is another fire-starting tool. Simply wrap the string of a bow—which you can make from a stick and cordage—around the spindle.

SURVIVAL TIP

If you have a steel knife, look for flint. It's a hard, gray rock that can create sparks when steel rubs against it.

Rub the spindle between your hands or pull your bow back and forth. With enough rubbing, you'll be able to create enough heat to start a fire.

HUNTING TOOLS

If you're in the wilderness and you need food, you may have to try hunting. You can hunt with the knife or spears you learned how to make earlier. You can also use hunting traps.

A trap is an object that's used to catch animals. Traps draw animals to them with food, or they're placed directly in an animal's path. There are traps that are built to fall on animals or to close down on a part of their body. Snares and deadfalls are popular traps that can be built from wood and cordage.

SURVIVAL TIP

Animal meat is a great source of the energy our body needs to survive. However, don't hunt more than you need. It's important to respect nature.

A large rock and a few sticks are all
that's needed to create a deadfall.
It's a simple—but useful—hunting tool.

TOOLS FOR COOKING

Once you have your food, you'll need tools to cook it. Eating uncooked meat can make you sick. Whittle a stick into a spear or skewer. You can use it to hold your meat over a fire.

Or tie your food to a metal rod, and place it over your fire using a stick on either end as support. Turn the meat to cook it evenly, and you'll have a great meal. These are just a few ideas. Some wilderness adventurers have created meat smokers out of giant leaves!

SURVIVAL TIP

Drinking is as important as eating. Fold large leaves into a bowl or cup shape to create a tool for collecting water.

The cooking tools mentioned here go back a long way. Long ago, people didn't have stoves or ovens, so they had to cook using tools taken from their environment.

GET TO WORK!

For thousands of years, people have made and used tools to survive. There are tools for cutting, tools for cooking, and tools for building. Without tools, we wouldn't be able to make fire or hunt. A tool can be anything from a simple rock to a handmade knife. They're all equally important.

Knowing how to make tools in the wilderness is an important survival skill. Take time to practice making different kinds of tools—you never know when you'll need them.

GLOSSARY

blunt: Not sharp.

challenge: Something that tests someone's abilities.

energy: The power to do work.

environment: The surroundings in which a person, animal, or plant lives.

fiber: A thread from which plants are made.

improvise: To create or do something without having prepared.

material: The matter from which something is made.

shelter: A place that keeps a person safe from bad weather.

situation: A series of events in which a person finds himself or herself.

skewer: A long piece of wood or metal used for holding food during cooking.

spear: To pierce. Also, a tool with a long handle and sharp pointed end.

terrain: Land.

wilderness: A natural, wild place.

INDEX

WEBSITES

Due to the changing nature of Internet links, PowerKids Press has developed an online list of websites related to the subject of this book. This site is updated regularly. Please use this link to access the list: www.powerkidslinks.com/wss/tool